You Took the Last Bus Home

YOU TOOK

BRIAN

THE LAST

BILSTON

BUS HOME

Unbound

First published in 2016 by Unbound
This edition published in 2017

Unbound
6th Floor Mutual House 70 Conduit Street London w1s 2GF

Typesetting by Bracketpress

Art direction by Mecob

A CIP record for this book
is available from the British Library

ISBN 978-1-78352-305-4 (trade hbk)
ISBN 978-1-78352-306-1 (ebook)
ISBN 978-1-78352-307-8 (limited edition)
ISBN 978-1-78352-492-1 (paperback)

Printed and bound in Great Britain by Clays Ltd, Elcograf S.p.A.

5 6 7 8 9

MIX
Paper from
responsible sources
FSC® C018179

For all the Bilstons

Dear Reader,

The book you are holding came about in a rather different way to most others. It was funded directly by readers through a new website: Unbound.

Unbound is the creation of three writers. We started the company because we believed there had to be a better deal for both writers and readers. On the Unbound website, authors share the ideas for the books they want to write directly with readers. If enough of you support the book by pledging for it in advance, we produce a beautifully bound special subscribers' edition and distribute a regular edition and e-book wherever books are sold, in shops and online.

This new way of publishing is actually a very old idea (Samuel Johnson funded his dictionary this way). We're just using the internet to build each writer a network of patrons. Here, at the back of this book, you'll find the names of all the people who made it happen.

Publishing in this way means readers are no longer just passive consumers of the books they buy, and authors are free to write the books they really want. They get a much fairer return too — half the profits their books generate, rather than a tiny percentage of the cover price.

If you're not yet a subscriber, we hope that you'll want to join our publishing revolution and have your name listed in one of our books in the future. To get you started, here is a £5 discount on your first pledge. Just visit unbound.com, make your pledge and type **lastbus** in the promo code box when you check out.

Thank you for your support,

Dan, Justin and John
Founders, Unbound

Contents

Introduction

You will either be reading this as an introduction to what you are about to read or in search of an explanation as to what you have just read. You may not even be reading this introduction at all, in which case the point, if indeed I was about to make one, is moot.

Regardless of your motivation for either reading or not reading this bit, I would like to take this opportunity to describe, in general terms, the key characteristics of the poems that you will encounter in this collection.

Firstly, **some of them rhyme**. And not just the kind of moody half-rhymes you may encounter in the work of my contemporaries, but proper, perfect rhymes. This is quite deliberate on my part. I do like a rhyme. But not all the time.

Secondly, to demonstrate my poetic versatility, **some of them do not rhyme**. These poems were harder to write as I had to select words from a much larger pool. It has been estimated that there are over one million words in the English language, and so hand-picking each word to go into a poem has proven to be something of a Herculean labour.

Thirdly, **there is variation in length and width**. Most of these poems have been shared in earlier, more primitive versions on social media, particularly Twitter. There are some which were written to be small enough to fit in a tweet. Other, more expansive efforts were photographed and posted up as pictures, grainy and indistinct like their author.

Fourthly, **many do not follow standard poetic forms and structures**. This stems from a deeply held conviction that expression is more powerful when rules are abandoned and that poetry needs to free itself from the shackles of the literary convention. That and the fact that I don't know what rules I am breaking.

There *are* pieces in here which I am not even sure are poems in any academic sense, and you will discover words written inside Venn diagrams, organisational chart structures, Excel spreadsheets and the like. I wrote them simply because they were different to preconceived notions of what forms poetry should be found in, and they were fun to write.

Fifthly, **some of them may contain jokes**. But not necessarily ones which are funny. I suppose that means I shall be disapprovingly exiled to the bleak, literary island commonly known as Light Verse with the expectation that I spend the rest of my writing career complaining about how I just want to be taken *seriously*. Well, I don't. I want to be taken unseriously, at all times, even when – perhaps *especially* when – I am writing about serious things.

Finally, **many of these poems are about every-day places and situations**: waiting for an online shopping delivery, going on a work 'awayday', staring at a mobile phone, taking the last bus home. They would often be partly composed while I was in the middle of these situations, either quickly thumbed into my phone or clumsily assembled in my head.

I suppose these are not *traditionally* regarded as being the stuff of poetry. But there is poetry to be found in anything if you look hard enough.

Brian Bilston,
March 2016

You Took the Last Bus Home

you took
the last bus home
don't know how
you got it through the door

you're always doing amazing stuff

like the time
you caught that train

The Ice Cream Vans

It has been warm this winter
so it was not until today

that I saw the vans begin
their slow rumble south –

startled into movement
by the early January frost

which had gathered softly
upon their windscreens

before waking them suddenly
as if from a night sweat.

I watch this strange procession
as it passes, a curious sight

suggestive of fun and funerals –
an ice-creamed cavalcade,

a cornettoed cortège
of lollies and 99s,

all pinks and whites
and Mr Whippy markings –

bound for North Africa.
Not all will make it.

And, as they pass by,
I hear the wayward chimes

of *Greensleeves*, *O Sole Mio*,
Half a Pound of Treacle,

for these are the songs
they sing to each other

as they start their journey
and I feel myself charmed

even though they do not
chime for me.

For We Shall Stare at Mobile Phones

Streets shrug as we roam back to our homes,
obstacle courses of lamp posts and cones.
For we shall stare at mobile phones.

Landmarks languish and attractions close;
statues, museums, cathedrals disowned.
For we shall stare at mobile phones.

Reading gets shelved, poetry and prose,
the dusty rebuke of neglected tomes.
For we shall stare at mobile phones.

Conversation falters, dries up, unflows,
feelings once said lie buried, unknown.
For we shall stare at mobile phones.

Yes, we shall stare at mobile phones,
when we're together and when we're alone.
For we shall stare at mobile phones.

And when we die, let us hope that they're thrown
into the pit with our crumbling bones.

This poem was sent from my iPhone.

A Surprise Ending

They say
we all have a book in us
but only a few
have two.

Like Howard,
who devoured
The Selected Plays of Noël Coward

but then,
to his surprise,
before his eyes,
he saw his abdomen distend
and it came out *Howards End*.

University Challenged

The Navier-Stokes equation governs
the behaviour of what form of matter?

Monday night, on the sofa,
slippers on, supper over,
hand resting upon my chin,
brow furrowed and leaning in,
my mouth shapes to form a word.
But nothing comes that can be heard.

Which two heteronyms are words used
to describe workers who have joined together
for self-protection, and a chemical compound
that has not dissociated electrically?

What IS a heteronym?
The opposite of a homophone?
I'm sure this is the kind of thing
I must have known once, though,
before my brain began to fur and slow.

On the TV it seems they all moved on
several minutes ago.

Alamogordo, the site of the detonation
of the first atomic bomb in 1945,
is situated in which US state?

I have been thinking
about Henderson's tie,
considering the sequence of its stripes,
and pondering why
anyone would choose to go
on national television
dressed as their father.

Perhaps Henderson would rather
it were nineteen seventy-three;
the tweed jacket with elbow patches,
and the glare of the studio lights
off his horn-rimmed glasses.

The rule of reaction called 'double displacement'
or 'ionic association' is also known by what one-word term?

I spend some time
wondering if Dugdale
has ever slept with Pratley
or whether she is put off
by his acne
and that funny little fist-pump he does
when he gets a question right.

I have just noticed Davies.
He has not said a word all night.

In cytogenetics, what term describes the entire
chromosomal complement of a cell which may
be observed during mitotic metaphase?

More minutes pass.
I only watch Davies now.
I long for the light of his buzzer.
But it is never him.
It's always another.

I sense his awkwardness
growing inside like a cancer,
the silence between question and answer.
I'm sure it's not that he isn't clever;
he is just a pause that goes on forever,

never right, never wrong,
going, going, going,
gong.

I turn the TV off
and put the kettle on.

In Praise of the Comma

How, great,
to, be, a, comma,
and, separate,
one, word, fromma,

nother.

Night at the London Palindrome

A hall.
I saw gig.
Was ill.
A-ha.

Carpe DMs

Doc Marten boots,
you take me back to my roots,
when you were in cahoots
with both of my foots.

You have style. You have sole
(air cushioned to make you hover),
with optional steel toe-caps
in case there's a bit of bovver.

Punks, poets, construction workers
all enlist you for their cause,
to tread upon carpets and concrete,
office and factory floors.

Dependably Manufactured!
Durably Memorable!
Doughtily Multipurposeful!
Diametrical Moccasins!

Carpe DMs!
The ultimate in utilitarianism.
To persuade me of otherwise
would be an act of futilitarianism.

Frisbee

Frisbee whizzing
through the air
above our heads,
over the sand,
into the water,
onto the waves,
out to sea.

You cried a lot that day.
Frisbee was a lovely dog.

Literal Thinking

The first time I remember seeing you
was when you fell off the scaffolding
and into the wet cement below.

You left quite an impression.

Later we met at Literary Sculpture class,
where we would fashion the great writers
out of wicker. Me: Joyce. You: Twain.

You really made your mark.

We only ever kissed once
but I recall that fateful bluster of a day
as if it were yesterday.

I was blown away.

Poem, Revised Draft

I had to write this poem again.
I left the first draft on the train
and now it doesn't look the same.

The original was a paean to Love,
to Truth, to Beauty. It soared above
the everyday and all that stuff.

It would have healed estranged lovers' rifts,
stilled the sands on which time shifts
and stopped the world before it drifts

further into quagmired crisis,
ended famine, toppled ISIS,
employed ingenious literary devices.

I tried my hardest to recall
its words and rhymes, the rise and fall
of the carefully cadenced crawl

through the English language.
But it caused me pain and anguish
for there was little I could salvage.

It certainly didn't end with a line like this.

Ping to My Pong

you put the sing in my song
i'll be the king to your kong
you are the bing to my bong
i wear my thing in a thong

Thirty Rules for Midlife Rebellion

1. Stack dishwashers in unruly ways.
2. Do not take part in 'dress down Fridays'.
3. Eschew quinoa and banish kale.
4. Burn your copy of the *Daily Mail*.
5. Do not use the tongs provided.
6. On escalators, stand left-sided.
7. Admire yourself in car wing mirrors.
8. Run in corridors, with scissors.
9. Avoid all weekend breaks in yurts.
10. Never wear Ramones T-shirts.
11. Pretend you do not like Adele.
12. Eat a packet of silica gel.
13. Do not watch golf at The Belfry.
14. Never ever take a selfie.
15. Do not accept food substitutions.
16. Ignore all products called 'solutions'.
17. Do not go for early morning runs.
18. Avoid the lure of Mumford and Sons.
19. Mix with people who are not like you.
20. Add a syllable to a haiku.
21. Put your darks in with your whites.
22. Do go gentle into that good night.
23. Destroy your Boots Advantage Card.
24. Treat *Top Gear* with disregard.
25. Finish your crossword by bedtime.
26. Do not sign up for Amazon Prime.
27. Take cover from all psychiatrists.

28. Do not read poems disguised as lists.
29. Dive-bomb into swimming pools.
30. And never EVER follow rules.

The Explosion

NEVER put a Minto
in a Vimto.
That's how the dinosaurs
became extincto.

Words

Words are absurd.

Words can stick in your throat,
particularly the ones
you can't get in edgeways.

Words can teeter on tenterhooks
on the tip of your tongue
(until someone comes to take them
right out of your mouth).

Sometimes you can even have a word in your ear.
A word in your ear!
If it was a long word, like *onomatopoeia*,
you might struggle to hear.

Words can be slurred.
Words can be blurred.
Words can be misheard.
And listeners deterred.

Words can fail you,
utterly.

Read My Lips

I don't need a lover
who's a looker,
just someone who knows
the shortlist
for this year's Booker.

Somebody who holds
a view on
Ian McEwan,
or is satanically well-versed
in Salman Rushdie

and who might find it cushty
to share pillow talk
about A.S. Byatt.

Yes, that would be a riot.

I could never judge a lover
by her cover,
and let myself be swayed
by make-up or a fancy hairdo;
not if she were intimate
with *À la recherche du temps perdu*.

To be clear, I'm not talking
Fifty Shades of Grey here,
but someone who knows their way around
the complete works of Shakespeare.

I would rip out my heart
and write her name upon it
if she might recite to me
his eighteenth sonnet.

So don't give me eyes
to get lost in,
I'd like a lover of Jane Austen
or an admirer of Joyce.

She could have the voice
of Donald Duck
for all I care
if she were prepared to share
her rare edition
of *Vanity Fair*.

Because something I've learnt
as I've got older
is that literature
lights up love
and makes it smoulder

and that beauty
is in the eye
of the book holder.

I Before E (Except After Sea)

For relief from the heat
I swam in the sea.
Dreid myself breifly.
Had freinds for tea.

No Hands Macpherson

'No Hands Macpherson',
they called him.

Partly for the way
in which he rode his bike
(with no hands)
and partly
because he had no hands.

The Heebie Bee Gees

He danced
like a man possessed
one fevered Saturday night.

He gave me
the heebie bee gees
and so I left the floor in fright.

Some blamed it
on the Boogieman
but it was a John Travoltageist.

Curriculum Vitae

PROFILE

A selfish, self-centred, self-effacing self-starter.
A team-playing, dragon-slaying, modern-day martyr.
A blue sky thinker whose ideas are a vapour trail.
A proven communicator with a kean eye for detial.

EXPERIENCE

POET — 2012–PRESENT

Duties included: being deluded,
finding myself from parties excluded,
writing sonnets on love and despair,
Netflix, and falling asleep in my chair.

VARIOUS POSITIONS — 1991–2012

Chartered Accountant. Lawyer. Cashier.
Building Site Lackey. High Grand Vizier.
Inhuman Cannonball. Scullery maid.
Skilled Chicken Sexer. Guitarist in Suede.
Postman. Dustman. Class A Drug Dealer.
Dog Trainer. Tea Strainer. Banana Peeler.
Batman. Batsman. Bowler. Head Chef.
Doing odd jobs for my Uncle Geoff.
Goalkeeper. Zookeeper. Dandelion Tamer.
Pilot. Hotelier. DJ. Boogie Blamer.

EDUCATION

UNIVERSITY OF LIFE — 1988–1991

My time at university saw diminishing returns.
Studied Scottish poetry. Got third degree Burns.

SCHOOL OF HARD KNOCKS — 1981–1988

School for me, I must confess,
proved an unqualified success.

INTERESTS

In my spare time, I like to ponder
the fragile silk of existence
as it hangs
like the industrious spider's
silver-sewn threads
and billows in the late afternoon breeze.

I also enjoy ten pin bowling and the films of Bruce Lee.

REFERENCES

Sadly, my references
have altered their preferences;
their words are harsh and
abhorrent.

Even mother and father
have said they would rather
not comment.

Scenes from a Railway Carriage

The silent stretch of fields in s—
The sudden surprise of a blackbir—
A ragged scarecrow stares b—
A plastic bag seized by natur—
An abandoned barn li—
Some houses.
Slough train station.

Twelve Haiku

INSTRUCTIONS
Please choose the haiku
which applies the most to you.
Choose two, get one free.

I
Subbuteo man.
Legs broken but re-glued twice.
A fragile sadness.

II
A leaf, desolate,
wind-blown, stuck to the back of
Bruce Forsyth's toupee.

III
A note left hanging
in the cold night air, dispatched
from a flugelhorn.

IV
Unclaimed bag revolves
on a lonely carousel.
Such a hopeless case.

V
Lonely, vacant box
in someone else's org chart.
Never to be filled.

VI
Imperfect haiku,
starts off quite well but ends one
syllable short.

VII
A tranquil puddle
disturbed by a sudden splash!
Clarkson's driving glove.

VIII
A semicolon
in a place where it really;
has no place to be.

IX
Reality show
contestant on a journey
back home to Skegness.

X

A smell which lingers.
Vaguely reminiscent of
Adrian Chiles' socks.

XI

The forlorn pathos
of an abandoned crossword
in a bin in Fife.

XII

A bag of Quavers,
offering cheesy comfort
yet steeped in staleness.

Compilation Cassette

It was about three weeks after we met
that I began work on that compilation cassette.
Each track the result of a deliberation worthy
of the Congregation of the Causes of the Saints,
subject to a process of veneration and beatification
before acceptance into the cassette tape canon.
It's a miracle it got made at all.

I can't remember now which songs made the cut.
There would have been no Country & Western,
(there was *never* any Country & Western)
but they would have shown me to be
discerning yet eclectic, both acoustic and electric,
vaguely exotic, mildly erotic, quintessentially quixotic
and other things I was not.

I don't know whether you ever played my cassette.
By the time I had posted it through your letter box,
you had already started going out with Colin Hancox.

He was good at rugby.

Acrostic Guitar

Got it for my seventeenth birthday.
Unreliant upon additional means of amplification.
Imperfectly tuned to reflect the flaws inherent in life itself.
Tank tops should be worn when playing it.
Accompaniment to songs of love, revolution, and farming.
Rattles with the ghosts of lost plectrums.

Bin Lorries

With the sureness of hearses, they
rumble through early morning towns,
oblivious of the slippered
footsteps on uneven pavements.
They loiter past every house:
all bins in time are visited.

Then children pushed out of front doors
and office workers who drum their
fingers on impassive steering wheels
observe the bleak, black voidance
of the week's detritus. *'The stench'*,
they whisper, as they turn away.

Borne off to sprawling landfill sites
and incineration chambers
or reincarnated, perhaps,
into other imperfect forms;
the rubbled, jumbled remains at
the end of their jagged journey.

And those who lie in beds unwoken
sleep troubledly all the same,
and dream of wasted days and nights,
filled with a lifetime's tawdry trash,
and wait and sleep and dream and wake
to the morning's insistent thrum.

Mixed Up

Poor *Brian* felt confused,
his *brain* out of order,
his *reward* was a prison,
without need of a *warder*.

For *Pam* was an anagram,
a crumpled *map* with no key,
his just *desserts*, he *stressed*;
he'd gladly *eat* her for *tea*.

But maybe she was *married*
or had some other *admirer*?
Yet hope's thin flame *resided*
in his heart; he *desired* her.

He was held *rapt* in a *trap*
and would think of her hourly.
She was *wordy*, she was *rowdy*;
she might come with a *dowry*.

He felt *angered*. *Enraged*.
World-weary. *Wired*. *Weird*.
Couldn't *declare* his feelings
until his head *cleared*.

He examined all the *angles*
and prayed to the *angels* above;
she gave him the will to *live on*
and he knew he must be *in love*.

Haiku for Doomed Youth

Cutting out pop stars
from last week's *NME* with
rock paper scissors.

Friday the 13th

Let's be clear,
for him Friday the 13th
held no fear.

He wasn't superstitious
(or even a little bit stitious)
and didn't view the day

as particularly suspicious,
or with the promise
of the unpropitious.

It was then that a black cat
crossed his path,
causing him to step on a crack

which made him stagger
under a ladder
and shatter a mirror

being transported
by a passing albatross,
who suffered fatal blood loss

from a shard
which had buried hard
into its heart.

He didn't think anything of it
until later that evening,
at a wine reception,

he found himself trapped
in a conversation
with Piers Morgan.

Duffle Coat

You were a one song wonder.
Don't know if you ever
made another.

Got made
NME single of the week.
It put the bubble
in my squeak
and the snap and crackle
in my pop.

I played it twelve weeks
non-stop
until the jingles
and the jangles
softened
the awkward angles
of what it's like
to be fifteen.

I kept the sleeve pristine.
I wore a duffle coat
all that summer.
Someone told me
you're now a plumber.

At the Intersection

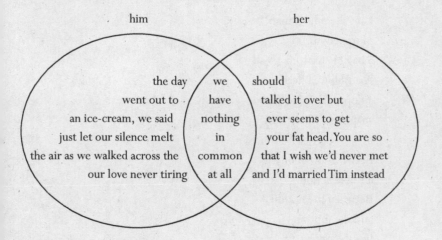

him

her

the day / we / should

went out to / have / talked it over but

an ice-cream, we said / nothing / ever seems to get

just let our silence melt / in / your fat head. You are so

the air as we walked across the / common / that I wish we'd never met

our love never tiring / at all / and I'd married Tim instead

The Pillow Man

I am the pillow man
plumped up
a bag of straw, that's all
A cushion of flesh
a floppy bean bag of bones
shapeless, silent, still

Between the thought
and the action
Between the notion
and the motion
lies the cat

For I am her dominion

Between the decision
and the reaction
Between the question
and the solution
lies the cat

She is very warm

Between the remote
and the television
Between the bookcase
and the book

Between the stairs
and the bed
lies the cat

For I am her dominion

For I am
For the cat is
For I am her

This is the way my day ends
This is the way my day ends
This is the way my day ends
Not with a bang but a whisker

The Power of a Homophone

'Sometimes the power of a homophone
comes out of nowhere and hits you,
just like being struck by a ten tonne truck,'
articulated Laurie.

Why Did the Chicken Cross the Road?

I saw the chicken cross the road,
deep-set in contemplation,
so I followed in the shadows
to end all speculation.

He sidled down an alleyway,
and then suddenly stopped dead
beneath a sign that gently swayed.
Upon it: *The Gag's Head*.

I heard a noise. *Knock-knock* it went.
'Who's there?' 'Just me. The chicken.'
I watched him quickly ushered in
and the plot began to thicken.

Through the window, I peered inside,
now intrigued about this place,
and the first thing that caught my eye
was a horse with a long face.

He held something black and white
which was also red all over,
and stroked a dog without a nose
from which came a dreadful odour.

And next to them, a big chimney,
smoking in front of his son,
and Pikachu who'd missed the bus
because nobody poked him on.

An Englishman, Irishman,
and Scotsman stood there in a group,
with an elephant in a fridge
and a breaststroking fly in soup.

The chicken got himself a beer
and joined their night of boozing;
to escape from this joke of a life,
made not of their own choosing.

I turned myself away from them
and decided I should split.
First rule of joke format club:
nobody talks about it.

Night Vision

To see at night
with extra clarity,
make sure the food
you eat is carroty.

And beware the dark
can seem much gloomier,
should you choose to make
your meal mushroomier.

Bonfire 451

I made a mighty bonfire
from remaindered copies
of *The World According to Jeremy Clarkson*

and saw the dance of sparks on
the face emblazoned upon
a thousand covers turn to flame,

spreading quickly across his name
and spine, until the pages caught
and raged in flickering fury.

Warming to the task, I threw
Kane and Abel by Jeffrey Archer
on the heap and the crowd grew larger

beneath the November night sky,
drawn in by the spectacle as
the paper crackled and smoke curled high.

Out of bags and rucksacks and pockets
came copies of *The Da Vinci Code*,
Twilight, Naomi Campbell's *Swan*,

Paul McKenna's *I Can Make You Rich*,
as the bonfire trembled and twitched
and turned fifty shades of orange.

Caught in the passing of a sudden breeze
were heard the shrieks of a hundred
ghostwritten footballers' autobiographies.

We stood back to admire our handiwork,
this funeral pyre of published inanities,
a bonfire of insanities.

How Much I Dislike the *Daily Mail*

I would rather
eat Quavers that are six weeks stale,
tie up the man bun of Gareth Bale,
listen to the songs of Jimmy Nail
than read one page of the *Daily Mail*.

If I were bored
in a waiting room in Perivale,
on a twelve hour trip on Network Rail,
halfway through a circumnavigational sail,
I would not read the *Daily Mail*.

I would happily read
the complete works of Peter Mayle,
the autobiography of Dan Quayle,
selected scripts from *Emmerdale*,
if it meant I didn't have to read the *Daily Mail*.

Far better to
stand outside in a storm of hail,
be blown out to sea in a powerful gale,
then swallowed by a humpback whale
than have to read the *Daily Mail*.

If I were blind
and it was the only thing in Braille,
I still would not read the *Daily Mail*.

A Brok n Po m

Upon b ing awok n
h found his k yboard was brok n.
Th ' ' did not work,
it drov him b rs rk,
h f lt lik a j rk.

So h w nt to s Louis .
Sh was ag r to pl a .

Sh was th b 's kn s.

Receptacles

It was a love that came together
through the use of receptacles;
for he had his beer goggles on
and she, her rosé-tinted spectacles.

How's Wally?

Paranoia stalks me
through the streets,

the park, the fairground,
the crowded beach.

I try to make myself
hard to see

because I think someone
is after me.

In a stripy shirt,
bobble hat, glasses,

I hide amongst
the unwashed masses.

Why they want me
I do not know,

but I keep on moving;
I must not slow.

So I wander lonely,
in a cloud,

choose the safety
of the crowd.

I just pray that
there'll never be

a Malthusian
catastrophe.

Sporkle

it is not the way you walk
it is not the way you talk
it is the way you wield a spork

queenly exponent of hybrid cutlery
you make my stomach
  utterly
    fluttery

one minute, your pronging
fills me with longing

the next,
you scoop to conquer

   it is driving me bonquers

elegant elision,
practised precision,

your spork
lights the spark
in my heart

rightly or wrongly,
I want you to
scoop me
then prong me

Roger's Thesaurus

In order to grow, expand, widen
his lexicological corpus,
Roger bought, acquired, purchased
a synonymopedia, a thesaurus.

Soon, presently, without delay,
he no longer ran out of things to say,
speak, utter, express, articulate,
give voice to, pronounce, communicate.

This was all very well, fine, great,
wonderful, super, terrific
but his friends, mates, pals thought him
boring, tedious, dull, soporific.

So let this be a warning,
an omen, a sign, a premonition,
it's all very well to show learning,
education, knowledge, erudition,

but here's a top tip,
a suggestion, some advice,
don't ever let it stop you
from being concise,

brief, short, clear, pithy,
succinct, compendious, to the point.

Breviloquent.

Too Much to Bare

Dr Augustus Meek
had a puritanical streak
through the streets of Preston.
Kept his pants and vest on.

Choreplay

Let's make love as soon as we are able
when the plates are cleared from the table,
the dishwasher stacked neatly
and the surfaces completely
wiped clean of crumbs and yolk.

We can leave the pans to soak.

Let's make our love fast and urgent
once I have bought some more detergent
because the backlog of laundry
is simply quite extraordinary;
we really should do it oftener.

I will also get some fabric softener.

Let our bodies writhe and manoeuvre
when I've finished with the hoover.
I know that it's rather late
but the house is in a state;
and our schedule has got off-kilter.

I think we need to change the filter.

Let our love be reckless, exciting,
after I have done the recycling;

the lilac sacks securely tied
and placed in the street outside,
careful not to cause obstruction.

And so begins the sweet seduction.

Orpheus in the Umbroworld

Orpheus descends
into the Umbroworld

of trackie bottoms
and replica tops,

ragged running shoes
and knee-length socks,

skeleton racks
of shell-suited overstocks,

and sidesteps
the slow shuffle of dead souls

with their tatty dreams
of Sunday morning goals,

deadly crossfield passes
and Hacky Sack skills.

He slays three-headed Cerberus
behind the tills,

who blows bubblegum balloons
from three sullen mouths,

and finds sweet Eurydice
wrapped up in sports towels.

Unlooking, he unravels,
unfetters, unfurls,

ushers her back through
the Umbroworld,

past gumshields and goggles
and tennis ball canisters,

under the watchful eye
of Nike and Adidas.

But, in the security screen
on the threshold,

the face of Eurydice,
he accidentally beholds

and she is suddenly gone
from him forever,

lost in the folds
of a thousand golf umbrellas.

The Day That Twitter Went Down

That day I got things done.
I went for a long run.
Played ping-pong,
wrote a song.
It got to number one.

That day I did a lot.
I tied a Windsor knot.
Helped the poor,
stopped a war,
read all of Walter Scott.

O what a day to seize.
I learnt some Cantonese.
Led a coup,
climbed K2,
cured a tropical disease.

That day I met deadlines,
got crowned King of Liechtenstein,
stroked a toucan,
found Lord Lucan,
then Twitter came back online.

Anthem for Unnamed Storms

Forget not those who came before:
the unmarked gales, the anonymous
squalls and unhumanised storms

whose howls haunt and batter
our memories still. Not for them,
a Met Office christening,

no blustery Barney, gusty Gertrude
or blowy, hapless Henry. For they
never knew what it is to be known.

But I shall batten down the hatches,
light the candle and give life
to the innominate from years long gone.

A late autumn day and I, aged five,
feel the sudden breeze as my mitten falls
into the lake. I shall call you Cedric.

A carrier bag in a 1980s supermarket
car park lifts into the air like a kite
and dances nervously in the wind. Sharon.

My carefully constructed quiff flattened
by the buffeting of Tim. A plastic chair
blown over on the patio by Colin.

The storms of my past. Eric. Patricia. Lesley.
Doris. Brandon. You have your names now.
Calm yourselves and be still.

Book Group

The last Thursday of every month was Book Group,
when the books would gather together
to discuss Graham.

'He has barely touched me; I am sure I am
only here so he can show off to his friends,'
complained *Ulysses*, in a stream of self-consciousness.

'Consider yourself lucky,' cried *Fifty Shades of Grey*.
'He's always got his dirty hands all over me.
Look at my cracked spine and turned down corners!'

'At least he's prepared to put you two on display,'
sobbed *Coping with Erectile Dysfunction* limply
from behind *The History of the Decline and Fall
    of the Roman Empire*.

'The problem isn't him, it's you,' declared the
    Oxford English Dictionary,
with meaning. 'You get too involved. With me,
it's just a quick in and out. We have an understanding.'

'That's all very well for you to say, pronounce,
    utter, articulate,'
muttered *Roget's Thesaurus*, who always had some words
    to add to the conversation.

Graham entered the room, carrying a box.

Dipping into it, he pulled out a slim, shiny metal object.

He stared at it all night, his interest kindled.

The books sat silently on the shelf.

Coquet

I put down my *Guardian*,
remove my cardigan,
other clothes follow
slowly,
sliding seductively
to the floor

I'm a snake shedding its skin,
peeling,
revealing,
on the hunt
for some healing

Garments slip,
I bite my lip
in anticipation
of emancipation

But then the doctor turns around and says,
'You can keep your underpants on, Mr Bilston.'

Smoking Jacket

He got himself a smoking jacket,
he thought it would amaze her.
But she just put a match to it,
and it became a blazer.

Bags

you have bags of bags

in your bags
you keep more bags
all bagged up
in bags for life

if there was a competition for number of bags
you would have it
in the bag

i don't know why you need so many bags
it's not as if you have anything to put in them

except other bags

No, You Cannot Borrow My
Mobile Phone Charger

Help yourself to whatever you'd like from my larder:
my stilton, my sherry – or my port, if you'd rather –
but no, you cannot borrow my mobile phone charger.

If you want I will read you an ancient Norse saga,
or dance naked in public to Radio Gaga,
but no, you cannot borrow my mobile phone charger.

Make me learn all the speeches of President Carter,
or force-feed me quinoa until I grow larger,
but no, you cannot borrow my mobile phone charger.

You can beg all you want but I'm not going to barter
because no, you cannot borrow my mobile phone charger.

Granny Smith

Want to know
what's under
that tough green skin?

Apply within.

Jessica Fletcher Investigates

Crushed to death.
No blood, no note.

Just a steel beam.
Girder, she wrote.

Love Excels

	A	B	C	D	E	F	G
1							
2		Let's	spread	ourselves	on	sheets	of love,
3		turn	our	data	into	poetry.	
4		Cells shall merge themselves together					
5		while you wrap your text	around me.				
6							
7		Apply ▼	a ▼	filter ▼	to our ▼	best ▼	bits, ▼
8		and	crunch	our	figures	without	compunction.
9		Our sum	is	greater	than	our	parts;
10		you	give	me	form	and	function.
11							
12		Let's	have	fun	among	the	formulae,
13		pivot	our	tables	now	and	often.
14		I	will	format	all	your	rows
15		and	you	can	total	my	column.

74

Busman's Holiday

I had always wanted to go
on a busman's holiday
so I saved up for ten years

and then five holidays
came along at once.

Paradise Not Regained

The retreat of a rented cottage,
bathed in late summer's shade.
Urbanity unfurls itself
in the seclusion of the glade.

Nature's tapestry surrounds me;
a timeless river flows through,
the towering forest comforts,
the sky dips in cloudless blue.

Inside, the considered furnishings
of the holiday home owner's dream:
cushion-piled beds, rustic kitchen,
the sofa of unsullied cream.

All immaculately conceived,
pure and clean, without marks on.
But then I see, on a bookshelf,
The World According to Clarkson.

Eden withers and dies around me,
forever more the holiday stained;
The satanic stumble, the fall from grace.
Paradise found, lost, never regained.

Running Wild

Returning to his old school
twenty years later,
he vanquished
childhood fears of chastisement
  by running
    in the corridor
      with scissors in his hand
and, so doing,
liberated himself from
the claustrophobic confines
of his cloistered conformity.

He did this
for approximately twelve seconds
before the tiger got him.

My Unbearable Politeness of Being

It's the same dilemma
each year, I find,
upon meeting a person
for the first time,

for how long
does wishing them
a Happy New Year
remain *de rigueur*?

Perhaps I blow things
out of proportion
but I tend to err
on the side of caution

so I've always
Happy New Year-ed
until October the third.

Pusher

The next time they came for me,
I was ready. Surprised them,
as they forced my head down
into the urinal, with a sonnet.
Smashed them like a bowl of eggs.

The demands changed.
Lunch money settled in my pocket.
Homework remained unstolen.
Instead, a request for a villanelle.
A haiku. A rondeau.

I was the don, a playground
dealer in dactyls and spondees.
Two lines of iambic pentameter
to get through double physics.
Cinquains snorted behind bike sheds.

Ballads kicked around at break.
A cheeky limerick to impress the girls.
Then one day a boy in the year below
OD-ed. An irregular ode apparently.
Nowadays I stick to novels.

Clive of Suburbia

Clive's a brass-knocker examiner,
a doughty door-hammerer,
selling Wikipedia Britannica
with suburban street stamina.

He goes from door to door.
His feet feel sore and raw.
He's just turned forty-four,
more or less (for less is more).

He's a doorstep smash-and-grabber.
A gilt-edged gift of the gabber,
he got the moves, he got the glamour,
he got more jabber than MC Hammer.

To Clive there can be nothing easier
than selling self-authored pseudo-academia,
fifty leather-bound laptops of Wikipedia,
with a month's free access to Virgin Media.

The Boogie Monster

You were always blaming things on the boogie.

The time you stayed out in the sun too long
and your speckles turned to freckles: the boogie.

The evening you admired the light of a full moon
only to trip and fracture your hip: the boogie.

Even those times which once seemed good
became named, shamed and blamed on the boogie.

I quite liked the boogie.
I didn't know why you had such a problem with it.

Morrissey's Quiff

His quiff
was stiff
from all the hairspray,
I dare say.

Thin Poem

this
poem
is
thin,
slim,
svelte,
has
no
need
to
tighten
its
belt

Subbuteo

They lie there as if in state,
green boxes transformed into tombs,
a taphephobiast's fearful fate.
A living nightmare looms.
A grave situation indeed.

Your hymns
will not stir the fallen
inside these curious coffins,
nor mend their
shattered, scattered
l i m b s.

All over the country,
in all of the attics,
lie these atrocities of neglect,
of athletics, rovers
and cities fanatics.

Those childhood cup dreams
gather dust,
no more the trophy
held aloft,
for the loft holds now
only atrophy.

The Offertory

She would go to church
every Sunday,
religiously.

Not to listen
to the bullshit
from the pulpit,
but to watch Ray
with the offertory tray
advance in style,
and wish it was her
he was taking
up the aisle.

And at night,
the curate
would contemplate
and take stock
of the romance
which blossomed
in his flock,
and live out
in his dreams,
their courtship,
vicariously.

The Problem of Writing a Poem
in the Shape of a Heart

He wrote a poem
in the shape of a heart to tell her
he loved her and that they never should
part. And that she was his sun and his stars and
his moon, and how he had dreamt that they might
marry quite soon. But she thought him stupid,
ugly and dreary and told him she loathed
him in practice and theory. And so
he went off to ponder the
words that she'd spoken,
and it was then that
he saw that his
poem was
bro ken.

Envy Not the Rich Man for I, Though Poor...:

Envy not the rich man his stocks and shares,
the offshore accounts, and his French au pair
who minds the kids when he's out on the piste
with the trophy wife he plundered from Greece,
and his city pad and country estate,
the mistress he keeps for when he works late,
his Jag, Bentley and Range Rover Evoque,
his Dom Pérignon, and Black Dragon smokes,
the island retreat of which he's so fond
where the Bahamian sun turns him to bronze.

For I, though poor, have him tied to this chair.
The night is still young. He hasn't a prayer.

Light Verse

I have a problem with light verse
and I worry that it's getting worse.
I find the weight quite hard to gaug e .
and so the words float up the p a g e

There are some w ay s to m ake them hold.
Words won't float off if they are bold.
Or if not sure what else to do
thenstickthemdownwithsuperglue.

Internet Shopping

It's amazing
what you can buy online nowadays,
she thought,
adding the Democratic Republic of the Congo
to her basket.

She still wasn't prepared
to pay the extra
for next day delivery, though.

Cuppa

No matter
if you're uppity
or you cause
a brew ha ha,

you will always be
my cuppa tea,
my steaming mug of cha.

You should know,
my darling Darjeeling,
only tea leaves
me feeling
this way.

You turn me
fifty shades of Earl Grey.

This may sound wrong
but I'll be your lapdog

if you'll be
my lapsang souchong

and that's
the oolong
and short of it,

the infusing,
confusing
thought of it,

but please
don't make
a sport of it,

because without you,
I am defunct,

like a biscuit
waiting to be dunked.

New Year Office Chitchat

How was your Christmas?
you ask

and I think of
the bloodstained rug

and the silent scraping
of the spade

in the garden
at midnight

and the wash wash
washing of my hands

and the dreams,
those endless dreams,

which haunt
the night-time

and smudge
their thumbprints

on the day
to come

and I reply
Super, thanks. Yours?

Frenemies

keep your friends close,
your enemies nearer,

and your frenemies
at a point equidistant

between your friends
and your enemies

Love Poem, Written in Haste
(with Autocorrect on)

O what Brave New Worm is this
that holes you, my sweet darting love?
I see you in the stairs that twinkle
up in the heavy above.

Your light shins down upon me
and sets my heart on fir.
You stir up my emoticons
and fill me with dessert.

I gazebo upon your lovely Facebook,
your rainy nose, sweet, unmissable,
the blue-greed eyes like limpet pools,
your petty mouse, juicy, kissable.

Come with meat, Angel of my Drums,
hold my ham, journalist into the night,
and together lettuce explore the worm,
over the horizontal and out of sigh.

A Chemical Romance

He would think about **Her** periodically,
a daily tab**Li**ng of her essential elements;
her radiated **Be**auty, her **B**lue **C**rystal eyes,
the **N**obility **Of** her unde**FiNe**d elegance.

Her **Na**tural **Mg**netism **Al**tered his state,
laid **Si**ege to his body, **P**unctured a lung,
Shattered his **Cl**avicle, burst his he**Ar**t,
bro**Ke** his jaw, in**Ca**pacitated his tongue.

She was the topic of his **ScienTi**fic enquiry.
He sought to **V**alidate his **Cr**aziness,
the inso**Mn**ia, his li**Fe Co**mpounded
(iro**N**ically) by in**Cu**rable la**Zn**ess.

Life without her would be as flimsy as **Ga**uze,
boringly bei**Ge**, harmful like **As**bestos in a jar,
Sedated, air**Br**ushed and romantically ban**Kr**upt,
distu**Rb**ing, mi**Sr**endered, unhappil**Y** bi**Zr**re.

He became u**Nb**alanced, e**Mo**tional and i**T**chy.
He felt **Ru**bbish and frequently diar**Rh**etic.
He was like a little la**Pd**og, padding along in **Ag**ony,
a mere ane**Cd**ote. But **In** deep. En**Sn**ared. Pathetic.

She rocked his Ka**Sb**ah, turned on his **Te**lev**I**sion,
mi**Xe**d up his metaphors, set his itali**Cs** bending.

He was taking a **B.a.** in the **La**nguage of Roman**Ce**;
he **Pr**ayed the course would have a happy e**Nd**ing.

If he were **Pm** he might **Sm**ite all his rivals,
castrate them like **Eu**nuchs, declare them wron**Gd**oers,
wish upon them **Tb**, **Dy**spepsia or c**Ho**l**Er**a;
he'd ou**Tm**uscle an**Y**body, mount them on skewers.

When he saw her, he would b**Lu**sh and be bas**Hf**ul,
not **Ta**lk of ho**W** his **Re**servoir was overflowing.
He'd speak of **Os**mosis, **Ir**rational numbers, anaba**Pt**ism;
his conversation was n**Au**ght if not thoroug**Hg**oing.

But lit**Tl**e did he know that she kept a scra**Pb**ook,
a **Bi**ble of the words he'd s**Po**ken she'd caught.
Atmology, o**Rn**ithology, the Scramble for A**Fr**ica,
all neatly t**Ra**nscribed, e**Ac**h and every **Th**ought.

And so it came to **Pa**ss one **U**nexpected day,
a dow**Np**our, a **Pu**ddle, a moment d'**Am**our seized,
the a**Cm**e of Cupid's Arrow (his kno**Bk**errie, **Cf**)
and our two hero**Es** from enser**Fm**ent are freed.

And that's where this periodic tale ends
(although there are still some more elements)
with chemistry found in words, not just labs,
and secret equations in love's eloquence.

Lollipop Ladies

They were there again.
The off-duty lollipop ladies,
hanging around the precinct,

like louts in lab coats,
looking for trouble.
We knew

it was the bus drivers
they were waiting for
but civilians

were not immune
from their threats
as they hurried by

or from a stick
casually outstretched
to induce

a stumble.
But it was their patch,
so what could you do,

won, at pyrrhic cost,
from the traffic wardens
earlier in the spring.

Some still had
the scars to prove it.
There was blood

in the doorway
of Dixons that day,
tickets and lollipops

lay scattered
like confetti
and shattered bones.

Divided by a Common Language

Americans,
I have news to report.

I have done the 'math',
you are one letter short.

You could borrow the one
from the end of 'sports'.

The Interview

First, how was your journey?
Have you travelled far?
Did you come by train?
Or by bus? Or car?
Or strapped to the handlebars
of your mother's mobility scooter?

What do you enjoy the most
about your current role?
The smell of the stationery
that you stole
when you thought no one was looking?
The canteen's plump wholemeal rolls?
The workload that you can't control?

Where do you see yourself
in five years' time?
In a mirror? A muddy puddle?
Or a chance reflection in a shop window
as you busk for pennies
whilst pedestrians bustle past,
eyes averted? And in twenty years?
Or thirty? Alone? Bitter? Betrayed?

What's the first record you ever played?
Do you ever wear pomade?
Have you ever felt *truly* afraid?

What makes you think
you are qualified for this position?
The showy Moss Bros suit?
The cheap aftershave that smells like Brut?

Tell me, if you were to divide
sixty-four by the square root
of the capital of Ecuador,
what year was the Franco-Prussian War?

What are your main weaknesses?
Women? Whiskey? Wednesdays?
How does this job fit into
the grand sweep of human history?
And have you ever wondered
who you *really* are?

How was your journey?
Have you travelled far?

Black Friday

Few knew what lay in store that Friday.

It started, as these things always do,
with the haberdashers
where reckless price slashers
offered ten per cent off
cerise beading trimming.

Soon the place was full to brimming.

As the prices lowered
the tension rose,
resulting in a bloodied nose
by the children's clothes.

In Winter Wear,
customers turned to scufflers
over discounted mufflers
and there was more fighting
amongst the Table Lighting
as a shopper got lamped
and then put in the shade.

There was carnage by the cardigans,
burnings in Home Furnishings,
a fracas near the nail lacquer,

not to mention the infamous
mascara massacre.

In Luggage, someone leaked mustard gas
and the worst case scenario
came to pass.
Thirty-five shoppers
malled to death,
lost their lives in the fray:
casualties of consumerism,
to be remembered on Black Friday.

Hear, They're and Everywear

I here that their everywear,
those people who don't know
there 'their' from 'they're'.

It where's me down,
they're choice of word;
there grammar should not be scene
but herd.

A Forest, Which Grew

a trail of parsnips along the floor
was all it took to lure
the sons out of their caravan door

where mumford was, i wasn't sure

bundling the sons out of my van,
i planted them in tubs of manure,
watered them daily,
played them the banjo
and ukulele,
and watched them grow
in the golden glow
of a late summer afternoon

gazed upon the long limbs
lazing up to an incipient moon,
the entangled bramble of beards immune
to the unforgiving snip
of the shears that prune

mighty sons of mumford,
fifty feet high,
stretching up
into the pale night sky

Ballad of the Ballot Paper

I spoilt
my ballot paper

gave it treats,
bought it sweets,
mooned around,
doted

and, in the process,
became hopelessly de-voted

The Occidental Tourist

A mistimed side-step and I was in amongst the cagoules,
clipboards and backpacks, too late to backtrack,
too hubristic to hack my way through the touristic horde

which tsunamis me around two Oxford colleges,
the Bodleian, and the Radcliffe Camera, pitches me
in and out the Pitt Rivers before we wattle and daub

our way to Stratford-upon-Avon for much ado about
bardic-related birthplaces and Monday-matinéed monologues,
striking north to Viking lands of here be minsters and

castles and dungeons and museums and botanical
gardens and monuments and Edinburgh cobbled passageways
and walking tours and bus tours and ghost tours and

coach rides and airports and aeroplanes and twelve-hour
flights and unfamiliar landscapes and customs and I end up
spending the next twenty years of my life as a rice farmer

in the Ishikari Subprefecture of Hokkaido in Japan.

The Waiting Room

For two hours she sat,
clutching the ticket
from the machine.

But then,
she'd been waiting
all her life
to be seen.

Eggbasket

She was told not to put
all her eggs in one basket

but with only one egg
and only one basket,

she wasn't really sure
what her other options were.

Unforeseen Consequences

I

wrote

a poem

on a page

but then each line grew

to the word sum of the previous two

until I started to worry about all these words coming with such frequency

because, as you can see, it can be easy to run out of space when a poem gets all Fibonacci sequency.

You Can't Judge a Book

you can't judge a book
by its cover
but neither can
you cover a judge
with a book

unless the book
is a foldy-out one
with a map or something

Love Is a Skin

love is a skin
that protects you,
a warmth that spreads
from the tips of your fingers
to your heart

sorry – not love –
glove, i meant glove

Toby

It would soon be January again.

She did not know
where the year had gone.

Eventually she found it
hidden away
in a shoebox,
under the bed,
along with 1997
and 2005.

Toby.

He had taken the best years of her life.

Upon Delivering a Lecture on the Work
of One Direction

I was invited to a convention
on the work of One Direction
and there delivered a paper
on the intersection of Nature,
Proust and Devon Malcolm
in their 'difficult' second album
and the influence of Mao Zedong
upon 'Live While We're Young'.

It was a talk of depth and texture
but in the middle of my lecture,
Professor Stephenson of Yale
shouted 'Bilston, you epic fail!'

Fall

she loved to catch
the falling leaves
in autumn

      she would
  sit
      and   wait
         until
    she

      cautumn

The Perils of Reading

We sought other delights
as *Wuthering Heights*
had really started to bore us

but my Penguin Classic
went all Jurassic
when Emily Brontësaurus.

Prometheus Uncreased

No one could press a shirt
like Percy Bysshe Shelley.
It said in a programme
I saw on the telly.

He would flatten with flair
like a hero Byronic,
which I suppose you could say
is a little ironic.

Parties

I am always
in the kitchen
at parties,

hiding
in the vegetable rack,

wondering
when it might be safe
to slip out the back.

We Are Books

I am a book.

But one of those books
with an aspiration beyond its station,
a pale imitation of Nabokovian narration.
Characterisation never the strongest,
I'm forever on the longlist,
always the prize-maid, but never the prize
(watch out for that plot-hole).

You are a book.

The Turko-Polish Technical Dictionary
of Hydraulic Engineering, to be precise.
You are far from concise
and run into three volumes
with online supplementary material
(including downloadable PowerPoint slides).
I have very little idea how to read you
or whether I should even try.

But still we sit side by side,
on the shelf,
our companionable silence
speaking volumes.

Lines Written Upon Arriving at a Holiday Cottage and Discovering the Lack of Reliable Wi-Fi

slow burning days drag by
as the smouldering fag ends of hours
turn themselves to ash

second-hand jigsaws
sleep on dusty shelves,
uncontrite at their incompleteness,

next to a well-thumbed
Robert Harris and the fortnight
stretches like old laddered tights

evenings drab with Scrabble
and the death rattle of Yahtzee dice
provide no substitute

for videos of piano-playing cats
instagrammed selfies, status updates,
Lionel Richie memes

instead this, the buffering
and the suffering and the shutters
which rattle in the wind

The Grammar Police

the grammar police got him

split his infinitive open
removed his colon
and left him lying commatose

the next day he was pronouned dead

full stop

Upon Awakening to the Sounds
of Distant Rumbles

He awakes from seasonal slumbers
to distant rumbles. A storm approaching,
perhaps, or the muffled guns
from the ghost of a war long since waged
upon faded fields.

The dawn chorus wakens the dead and
rattles the brain as the backstreet clatter
recedes into murmured memory and the
awful truth emerges. Bin day! The revised
Christmas holiday collection schedule.

Thoughts fly unbidden to the rooms
of recycling, Pennines of packaging,
glaciers of glass, corridors of cardboard
and cartons, growing, overflowing,
silently creeping up the staircase, across
the landing, clawing at the bedroom door.
The horror! The horror!

He lies there and tries to collect himself.

Ode to a Weather Girl

I write you poems
and send you flowers

you give me hailstones
and scattered

Morrissey's Fridge

Morrissey was filled
with sudden self-doubt
as he shut his fridge door;
did the light never go out?

In the Departure Lounge

In the departure lounge,
she drew him near,
then softly whispered in his ear,
not words of parting's sweet, sweet sorrow,

but DON'T FORGET THE BINS TOMORROW.

This is One of Those Poems
Without Any Rhymes

This is one of those poems
without any rhymes,
of the kind you may read
in the *Sunday ~~Times~~ Telegraph*.

For the *real* poet, you see,
rhyme's deleterious,
when you want to be seen
as poignant and ~~serious~~ profound.

Rhyming is childish and trivial,
and it smacks of the frivolous.
But I'll throw in some half-rhymes
of which you may be ~~oblivious~~ ignorant.

This is also one of those poems
that ends with a ~~metaphor~~ simile,
like the silence of writing paper,
untouched in the letter drawer.

You Are a Map

In bed, my fingers trace your contours,
caress the lines from coastal margins,
slide along secluded pathways

and linger in hidden beauty spots,
before a gentle incline leads them
to the peaks of two majestic hillocks,

separated by a narrow ravine,
which I follow down, down, until
scrubland arrives as a surprise,

and gives way to enchanting forest.
I prepare to plunge into the interior
but then I am told to turn off the light

and so I carefully fold
my scale 1:25 000 Ordnance Survey OL4 Map
of *The Lake District: North-western area*,

including Keswick, Cockermouth & Wigton,
before placing it back in my bedside drawer,
alongside my pipe, nail clippers and loose change.

Haiku #478629

as he left the train,
he remembered to take all
his longing with him

Australia

A photo. 1977.
Me, on a beach in Devon,

digging a hole
down to Australia;

a project always
doomed to failure.

Although the photo
has begun to fade,

the disappointment
of that day has stayed

and I often replay
the mistake I made:

I really should have used
a bigger spade.

Your Search Returned No Results

I googled 'corporate profiteering'
but, with so few results appearing,
I wondered if I'd made an aberration
so I changed my search term to 'evasion'
but, again, I must have lacked the knack
for Google gave so little back.

For the avoidance of doubt and delusion,
I tried 'government big business collusion',
only to reach the same conclusion.

Perhaps there's a problem
with their algorithms,
or their coding needs
some more revisions.

Or they just found it all too taxing.
Next time, it's Jeeves I'm asking.

Reach out to Me

Reach out to me, reach out, reach out,
my calendar is up-to-date.
Let's meet up and move the needle
(although I have a hard stop at eight).

Drill down with me, drill down, drill down,
and under spreadsheets we shall dive,
pluck at the ripe, low-hanging fruit,
let's innovate and synergise.

Align with me, align, align,
explore our many moving parts.
We shall think outside the box
and get it down on your flip charts.

Deploy with me, deploy, deploy,
your assets quite considerable.
Leverage them along the way
to achieve our core deliverable.

Please Sing to Me Your Songs of Sweet, Sweet Love

Please sing to me your songs of sweet, sweet love,
let your music drift upon the breeze.
Or write me a sonnet straight from the heart
and carve the lines into this oak tree.

Or proclaim a constitution of love
and make your rules and principles clear.
Or if time is short to write such words,
whisper soft, hushed words in my ear.

Or scrawl something down on a post-it note,
you really don't need to think too hard.
Or if you have got a spare postage stamp,
you could always send me a postcard.

Or leave a phone message with my mum
(treble four seven nine double three)
as I've not heard from you in fourteen years
and I think you may be avoiding me.

Kiss

Gimme a kiss, a smooch,
a snog, a smacker.

Light up my lips
with a lusty firecracker.

Please don't ignore this;
let us conjoin
our *labia oris*.

Because I'm a sucker
for the way
that you pucker.

I hope
that our lips
get stucker and stucker.

So let's osculate now,
I can't help myself.

Oh, sorry,
I thought
you were somebody else.

Life: A Record

Polyvinyl chloride disc
with modulated spiral groove,
you're up to scratch,
you're prone to snap,
your pop's crackle makes me move.

You turn the tables,
you make me spin, your company is bliss.
I love you thirty-three and a third more times
than any compact disc
(and forty-five times more
than a download
from an online music store).

Digital is clinical,
cuts air like a surgeon's knife,
but vinyl has the touch, the feel,
and surface noise of life.

Selfie Stick

The modern fixation
upon the selfie,
I find not natural,
normal nor healthy.

Too much of the ME,
the MYSELF and the I,
not enough of the where,
the how or the why.

Selfies are senseless;
I'd much rather snap
the them and the those,
the what and the that.

Eager stroker of ego.
Photographic spam.
Bedroom or bathroom,
I click *ergo* I am.

Narcissistic reflections
in camera phone glory.
If a selfie could vote,
then it would vote Tory.

A Little Light Verse

How many
poets does it take to change
a lightbulb? Five. One to describe
the essence of its fluorescence, the light
which can turn darkness to unshaded starkness,
or gently summon shadow-furniture to silhouette soft,
silkened walls. Another to complain how the light bulb is
a poor substitute for sun or moon upon which the love-sick
lover might croon. One who will try to conjure up the crackle
of electricity as it flows through the filament and meets the
resistance it craves in order to make its sudden, startling
conversion on the road to domesticity. That poet will use
phrases such as luminous efficacy and tungsten trioxide
with the confident abandon of the polymath. Essential
to the operation is the poet who then shifts from
science to metaphor and presses the mental
switch which heralds the dawning of a new
idea, the eureka moment, and which, in
its turn, illuminates the human
condition and justifies the
continued existence of
poets in the first place.
And finally the poet
who goes to B&Q,
buys the lightbulb,
and returns to
his garret and
screws the
damn thing
into the
socket.

Untitled

She didn't know
who had written
the poem
she'd stumbled upon.

All she knew
was that it went on
anon.

Plane Verse

Dedicated to the passenger in front of me

When
  you
    recline
      your
        seat,
          it is difficult
          for me to eat

Anthem for Doomed Ruth

It was Ruth's own fault,
to tell you the truth;
she smoked like a chimney
and then fell off the roof.

Haiku Horoscopes

ARIES
your attempts to breed
male sheep have unexpected
ramifications

TAURUS
your luck starts to change
when into your life comes a
dark handsome strangler

GEMINI
Mars enters the sphere
of concupiscent Venus
not sure what that means

CANCER
you realise that
all horoscopes are nonsense
feel crabby all week

LEO
your hair turns curly
and you have a surprise hit
with When I Need You

VIRGO
the crowds gasp at your
Cliff Thorburn and Doug Mountjoy
impersonations

LIBRA
you fail to return
all the letters you borrowed
from the library

SCORPIO
reading horoscopes
in the newspaper, you bump
into a lamp post

SAGITTARIUS
you break with your strict
Sagittarian diet
and eat a Virgo

CAPRICORN
you decide to stop
thinking about anagrams
and sort out your file

AQUARIUS
you read a haiku
horoscope in this book but
it tells you nothing

PISCES
nightclub visit fails
you find there is no one to
pick up the Pisces

Whither Spoons?

Whither the spoons in my cutlery drawer?
Of spoons it is empty but it used to hold four.

I checked the dishwasher and I scoured the floor.
Then I scoured it again just to be sure.

Whither the spoons in my cutlery drawer?
Of knives and forks, I have plenty in store.

But what use is a knife except as a saw?
And what good is a fork except as a claw?

Whither the spoons in my cutlery drawer?
For scooping and stirring, it's the spoon I adore.

And should you ever look up at the shallow-bowled moon,
just think of the poet who perished for want of a spoon.

The Importance of the Oxford Comma

Owing to ambiguities caused by its omission,
the Oxford comma became the subject of a petition
raised by serious serialists desperate to ensure
its use was to be mandated in lists of three or more.

Signatures flooded in from across all of society;
never had they expected to see such variety.
Who would have thought that those in favour
would have had such a diverse, democratic flavour?

There were the investment bankers, the robbers and thieves,
as well as the politicians, the greedy and venereally diseased.
There were the footballers, clowns and less mentally able,
alongside the poets, unemployed and emotionally unstable.

Plus Simon Cowell, a drug fiend and a trafficker of human organs,
and the sexual deviants, Jeremy Clarkson and Piers Morgan.
Such was the range of names that the list did constitute.
Oh, and the Queen, a well-known madam and a prostitute.

Lapse

Chores were neglected,
dirty dishes stacked,
because people
had cats
who sat
on their laps.

Careers were stalled,
all plans got scrapped,
because people
had cats
who sat
on their laps.

Whole cities crumbled,
economies collapsed,
because people
had cats
who sat
on their laps.

Aliens invaded,
Earth got attacked,
but the people
just sat there
with cats
on their laps.

The Chelsea Flower Show Massacre

There was death amongst the daffs
the day Fleur took her secateurs
and ran amok through the flock

of haughty culturalists
in the Chelsea gardens
without so much as a beg your pardon.

Roses were red, violets were too,
ears were sheared, nosegays chopped,
toes trimmed and green fingers lopped,

as Fleur took the lawn
into her own hands
and mowed them all down.

Even the failure of Lady Pru's azalea bed
became overshadowed
by the trail of dead.

Herbaceous borders
filled up with her slaughters
and there was carnage in the carnations,

annihilation amidst the anemones,
hysteria in the wisteria,
nastiness in the nasturtiums.

No one could remember a flower show bloodier;
if only it had been nipped
in the buddleia.

Languish School

bed-filled days
    of tea, toast and
      truancy

they spoke
    the languish of love
      fluently

Haiku #64471

I am excused from
walking around church graveyards
on religious grounds

Invincible Vince

The day he got
the neck brace,
life changed for Vince

and he's never really
looked back since.

Every Song on the Radio Reminds Me of You

Every song on the radio reminds me of you.

'Anarchy in the UK' plays and I think about the time
you led a bloody but ultimately unsuccessful
anarcho-syndicalist uprising in Merthyr Tydfil.

'Bohemian Rhapsody' comes on and I remember
the episodic, integrated, free-flowing work
you composed whilst holidaying in the Czech Republic.

'Like a Virgin' reminds me of the afternoon
your new Virgin Media TiVo box was installed
and you touched it for the very first time.

A Beatles song blasts out and I recall those stupid
bloody Tuesdays when you would sit on a cornflake
in your corporation T-shirt and wait for the van to come.

Other memories fly to me across the radio waves.
Your strange, wide-ranging CV: private dancer,
waitress in a cocktail bar, boxer, lineman for the county.

The evening you let the dogs out. That party with
a special atmosphere. The year you missed my birthday
because you were sat in a tin can far above the world.

Little wonder I still think about you most days;
you and your beautiful, bright, sexy, gypsy,
Bette Davis, brown, green, baby blue eyes.

Clarkson Apologist

Reader, please beware
of the Clarkson apologist.

Here's how to find
if there's one in your midst.

He will tell you
that global warming does not exist.

He will talk about his little lady
then claim he's not sexist.

He will illustrate homosexuality
through the limpness of a wrist.

He will talk about the two world wars
and then clench his right fist.

He will bemoan the bloody immigrants
of which his country consists.

He will drive home every night
in his Range Rover pissed.

I could go on
but I'm sure you get the gist.

Melancholy Communion

When the wafer
began to chafe her

and the wine
said she had no class

she knew
things had reached
a critical mass.

Not Her Cup of Tea

just when
she thought
it could get no worse

she saw him
put milk
in her teacup first

Penned Up Emotion

'The pen IS mightier
than the sword,'
she roared,

squirting ink
into my eye

and stabbing
the nib
into my thigh.

'Life Is an Inspirational Quote'

Every day is a second chance.
And each day a festering boil to lance.

Paint the sky and make it yours.
I'll add this fun task to my long list of chores.

Imagination is more important than knowledge.
It helps me pretend I made it through college.

Be positive and turn your can'ts into cans.
Then watch my cans carted off in recycling vans.

What doesn't kill you makes you stronger.
It is hard to think of a quote that is wronger.

It is never too late to be what you might have been.
I gave up believing that when I was fourteen.

Life is so much brighter when we focus on what really matters.
That's assuming my dreams are not already in tatters.

You're in control. Be the change you wish to see.
I struggle to find change for a cup of tea.

A beautiful life begins with a beautiful mind.
In a world full of misery, it's not so easy to find.

Treat life like a trusted and old faithful friend.
Why not? But SPOILER ALERT: we all die in the end.

The Pedents' Revolt

Its not verry eazy being a pedent
correcting others' mistakes all daylong
My freinds and me are totally sic [sick]
of seeing gramma witch has gone wrong.

'Whom are these language offenders',
'could it be that I maybe one, to'?
Their ignorant; stupid, and careless:
off language they have'nt a clue.

They're speling is compleetly embarrasing
its' so amature, wired, and, abserd,
applying neither thought or intelligence –
to a dictionary they should of refered.

Writing there awkwardly formed sentences,
participle clauses remain dangled.
Just one less mistake each would have the affect
of making our language less mangled.

Lamina: A Palindromic Poem

A mall. As it is.
God!
Was it a cat I saw?
Dogs?
It is a llama.

If Your Heart Was an Org Chart

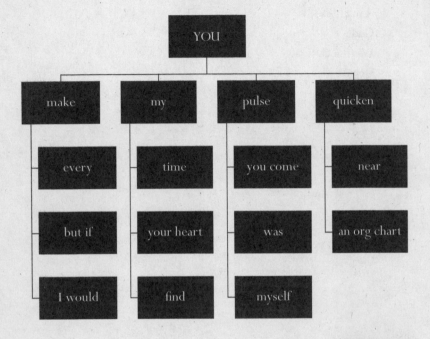

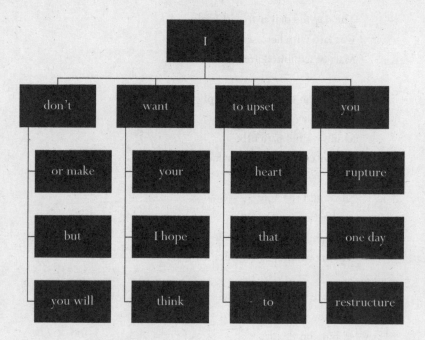

The Great Famine

The day the driver from Ocado
was late with her escargot,
Margot exhibited great bravado.

She had an insight into the plight
of the starving of Africa
as she waited patiently
for her celeriac and paprika.

She could see how
civilizations might fail
through focaccia gone stale
and for want of some kale.

And she thought to herself sadly
of those who sat drably
sipping on the dregs
of last night's Chablis.

With some charity or other,
she set up a small direct debit
and then stoically rustled up
a smoked haddock rarebit.

Clowns

Know this: those commuters
causing commotions on locomotions
with their funny fold-up bikes,
the vélo origamists of the vestibule,
are out-of-town clowns.

Their bags do not house laptops
or dossiers of documents,
but wigs and whistles, red noses,
hand buzzers and balloons,
water-spraying carnations, outsized shoes,
giant toothbrushes, chickens.

Follow them out of the station,
post-disembarkation.
Observe the nearness of their feet
to the saddle as they straddle
their bicycles and comically pedal
through London street puddles,
and peddle their selection
of slapstick services
to city centre circuses.

Beards

Beards grew on men's faces,
inched past belts and braces,
slithered over shoe laces,
spread across floors,
crept under doors,
stretched across streets,
became entwined and entangled
at all kinds of angles
until the ground disappeared,
drowning in beard.

Oceans got clogged
and mountains hogged
by the hirsuteness
that took rootness
as attempts to halt
the barbate bombardment
proved fruitless.

No glimmers of hope,
no trimmers could cope,
the vanity of humanity's
destruction impending;
a hairy tale ending.

Name Calling

Some names like Beauchamp,
get mispronounced
unless you teauchamp,

thought Niamh Cholmondley,
glolmondley.

Logomachy

To say that Damian
was sesquipedalian
would be an understatement
for there was no abatement
in his capacity for loquacity
nor lack of temerity
in his pursuit
of verbal dexterity.

It was precisely this pomposity
mixed with verbosity
which made him describe
Kieran Thomas as 'crepuscular'.

Kieran Thomas was also more muscular.

Damian nursed his black eye
and hoped Kieran
might be struck down with
pneumonoultramicroscopicsilicovolcanokoniosis.

Fluff

every evening,
for twelve years,
i would contemplate
my navel,
a nightly session
with my knotted
depression
in which
i would inspect
the cleft
to see what the day
had left

the daily deposit
would be scraped out
and stockpiled
into shoe boxes
until i had enuff
of the stuff
to knit you a scarf
of scraped fibres,
a lint-stitched muffler,
a belly button
fluffler

Desemicolonisation

Following the Pedants' Revolt,
it was clear the semicolons had to go.
Nitpicking sticklers sickened
by the centuries of their abuse,
misuse and misplacement
oversaw their displacement overseas.

Sentenced to de-sentencing,
they found themselves deported
to semi-colonies where
they could do no further harm.
Related clauses were reunited
or sadly, in some cases, split up.

Occasionally rogue semicolons
would still be found; in a newspaper;
an obscure monograph; a badly-written poem.
The perpetrators would live in fear
of the knock at the door and
the heavy boots of the grammar police.

Sometimes these authors would
suddenly disappear, mysteriously,
before they had even fini

Suspicion

The only thing Clive
ever carried in his briefcase
was a cheese and pickle sandwich.

Nothing unusual about that, perhaps,
but the other ants in the colony
still regarded him
with suspicion.

Origami

your love of origami
was uncontrolled

for reasons which were
manifold

but it soon decreased,
began to irk

what with all that
paperwork

Missing the Moon

life is all darkness
since you left
as if the moon
had gone missing
from the night sky
and left an absence,
a lunar lacuna

oh, hang on, forgot to open the curtains

Her Universe

She gazed up into the night sky
with intensity
and pondered the immensity
of the observable universe.

Space seemed so spacious,
forty-six billion light years in radius,
with recent astronomical analyses
suggesting one hundred billion galaxies
and stars numbering
three hundred sextillion
(give or take a few thousand billion).

Even if she set off soon,
a walk to the moon
would take three thousand days.
It would be sheer lunacy.

The universe held her spellbound
in its unimaginable boundlessness
until the phone rang
and she left the balcony
to go back inside
her one-bedroom flat in Croydon
to answer it.

Malcolm

Malcolm was a maverick
and would always have a trick
or two up his sleeve,
should he ever meet
the nous-less and naive,
he'd bob and weave
and stitch them up a treat.

Malcolm was a chancer,
a dancer, a Bengal lancer,
a ducker, a diver,
a scamp and a skiver
who'd steal the robes
off the back of a Lady Godiva
if you gave him a fiver.

Oh, Malcolm.

Wallycobbles

i remember the moment
when my collies
began to wobble
as if it were yesterday
which it was
give or take a year
or two

it came as quite a shock
until that point
they had always seemed
of steadfast
and sturdy stock
hardly worthy
of a tremor
or a tremble
but solid
solid as a rock

i presented them to the doc
parting his paperwork
to let them rest
quivering
and shivering
atop his pockmarked desk

he gave me
the heebie-jeebies
in a jamjar
saying
take two before breakfast
with a glass of wine
closely pursued
by two more
during newsnight

but not the bit when
the next day's papers
get perused

now they're as good as new

4' 37"

[The above poem is a homage to John Cage's experimental composition, *4' 33"*. Mine is a bit better, though, as it's four seconds longer (but only if read at the right pace). For best results, please approach this poem from the right hand side, in a mood of sullen indifference, whilst drinking a glass of Fentimans Ginger Beer.]

Needles

                    I
                  wrote
                a poem
              in the shape
            of a Christmas
          tree but then forgot
        to water it and only a few
                   days
                   later

                  there
          were
                              words
      all
                    over

            the   carpet

Little Poems

You would write
little poems for me,
and scatter them
around the house,
like unexpected confetti.

Elliptically cryptic
in construction,
your notes of seduction
defied further
deduction.

2 tins toms, read one,
Cuc x 3, caulie, bread rolls.
Dead Sea Scrolls
would be decidedly
more easily
deciphered.

I came to adore
these *lettres d'amour*,
and would secretly clamour
for their post-it-note
glamour.

Boiler on blink. Phone man,
said another.
Dinner in dog,
whilst perhaps
not the prettiest,
was one of your pithiest.

Prosaically profound,
part-Ayres, part-Pound,
your poems
would confound.

I hate you
and I hate your stupid face.
I am leaving you.
was you
at your pinnacle,
so crisp and so clinical.

Such a shame
you disappeared
shortly after that.

The Unbearable Lightness of Boing

I didn't hear you coming,
you got me good and proper

when you knocked me to the ground,
riding your spacehopper.

Things I Would (and Wouldn't) Do for Love

I would do anything for love.

Wear a hat,
do the dusting,
stroke your cat,
read Augustine,

but i won't do THAT
because that's disgusting.

Haiku #1

i don't really
know what a haiku
is

Ode to a USB Stick

Eighty-five per cent of people
a recent survey found,
first try to insert you
the wrong way around.

Paul Young

it was quite by accident
that i discovered paul young
in the garden that morning,
living under a hat

he appeared to have
made himself quite at home there
although he admitted
to periods of abject loneliness

i would visit him daily,
feeding him turnips,
the ends of which
he would store in his turn-ups

upon arriving, he would beg me
to stay for good this time
but having other things to attend to,
i never did

i did enjoy
the feeling of him being near, though,
so every time i went away,
i would take a piece of him with me

then one day, to my dismay,
i lifted up his hat and found

there was nothing left of him
for me to take

in a rage, i tore his playhouse down
before going inside to stroke
my cyndi lauper

You Stitched Together the Pauses

you stitched together
the pauses

from old, discarded
Harold Pinter

plays

until you had made yourself

a
blanket

of

silence

The Poet Laurie Ate

The poet Laurie ate
was Alfred, Lord Tennyson,
whom he found rather tough
although less so than venison.

The Correct Attire for Yoga

never do yoga
dressed in a toga

always wear
a leotard

check first
it is not a leopard

or your life
will be placed
in jeopard

y

Jewel

I can picture the exact moment
that we began to grow apart.
The usual Thursday kickabout,

the mistimed challenge, the boot
jack-knifed down upon my own,
the mumbled apology,

and the game continuing
around us. Back in the dressing room,
I looked for signs of damage

and although you looked
no different,
I knew that you were.

That night in bed, to prove me right,
your transformation, as subtle
as a reading lamp, began.

It was an unremarkable beginning.
A blanched greyness spread
across the nail, like a bland surprise,

as if the blundering ghost
of that tackle
had come back to haunt you.

In the days that followed
your true colours
began to shine through,

angry reds and bruised purples
competed with each other
before settling into an uneasy truce.

I would rush home each evening,
shoes and socks strewn across the hallway,
and inspect you,

to see what new hue you had become
and to run my fingers over
the contours of your newly-formed ridges,

as brittle as life itself.
They were bittersweet times
and all the while, the nascent nail

was growing and pushing,
undermining, overwhelming,
and toe's company, three's a crowd.

Our parting when it happened
came suddenly. The sun shining down,
a foot raised up from the sea,

and there the usurper
but not the usurped,
presumably washed away in the surf.

I still dream about you sometimes:
a beach-combing boy, looking for treasure
amongst the pebbles and shells,

his eye caught by an unexpected gleam
in the sand, and something both splendid
and mysterious is gathered up

for his collection: an Ionian jewel.

The Crocs of the Matter

the one crime worse
than wearing crocs
is wearing crocs
with socks

Tony

Of all my mates,
Tony was the pick of 'em.
He knew loads
about Tanita Tikaram.
Like that she was
from Basingstoke.

Tony. Amazing bloke.

Love Amongst the Dominoes

When Janice walked out
of his dreams
and into the saloon bar
of The Sparrow and Sickle
that domino-fuelled Thursday night,
Bob knew it was love at first sight
for he felt his blood thicken,
his pulse quicken,
damn near choked on his chicken
in a basket.

Janice-stricken,
Bob was a shadow
of his formless self,
no longer the doyen
of the domino domain
(for that was now Ken).

Tiles clacked with a fatal distraction.

As Bob watched Janice
sidle over to the jukebox
he imagined her
supplicant and supine,
until he heard her put on
'Walking on Sunshine'.

Bob was held in thrall no more
and he returned to the game.

For Bob there were some things
that love could not withstand.
Katrina and the Waves being one
(another, KC and the Sunshine Band).

A NIGHT ON THE TILES

198

AS HE PLANNED, A NEW ATTACK, SHE HOPED, HE WOULD PEEK, AT HER RACK.

Haiku #298610

There once was a young
limerick from Kew who turned
into a haiku.

Poetry Books Offer

Here's an offer
on Romantic poetry
that won't cost you the earth:

BYRON GET ONE FREE
if you want
your Wordsworth.

Lady Philately's Lover

She would invite him in
for secret binges.

He would lick his finger
then moisten her hinges.

POLICE NOTICE: Schrödinger's Cat

WARNING: Schrödinger's cat,
much-feared feline psychopath
and philosophical paradox,
has broken out of his box.

The four-legged ex-captive
is thought to be radioactive,
and quite possibly armed.

A number of creatures
have already been harmed;
none are likely to survive.

REWARD FOR CAPTURE: £100.
WANTED DEAD AND ALIVE.

Stack

forgive me

i did not mean
to stack
the dishwasher

in such
an inefficient manner

i never was
much
of a planner

Robert Frost's Netflix Choice

An action thriller
with Liam Neeson
or a post-apocalyptic
world forsaken?

Decides upon *The Road* not *Taken*.

Refugees

They have no need of our help
So do not tell me
These haggard faces could belong to you or me
Should life have dealt a different hand
We need to see them for who they really are
Chancers and scroungers
Layabouts and loungers
With bombs up their sleeves
Cut-throats and thieves
They are not
Welcome here
We should make them
Go back to where they came from
They cannot
Share our food
Share our homes
Share our countries
Instead let us
Build a wall to keep them out
It is not okay to say
These are people just like us
A place should only belong to those who are born there
Do not be so stupid to think that
The world can be looked at another way

(Now read from bottom to top)

No Laughing Matter

My mate Geoff
tickled a bloke
to death.

Four weeks after,
he got charged
with mans'laughter.

Fifty-One Words for Rain

It is said the Eskimo
has fifty words for snow,
but the British brain
holds fifty-one for rain.

It must be all those
Bank Holiday weekends
of peering through rain-spattered windows
to see the pittering and pattering,
the spitting and splattering,
the spotting, stotting and spithering,
the showering, sprinkling and tinkling.

Or holidays in Scotland,
with their dreich days of drizzle,
the smirring and the sneesling,
the raffing and the roosting;
and the misery of long, misty walks
in the mizzle.

It's best to batten down the hatches
to hear the haar and the hammering,
the haggering and the huthering,
the drumming and the thundering.

Because inside you are safe
from the risk of being struck

by buckets or stair-rods
or pitchforks or chair legs
or from the pelt of cats and dogs.

It never rains but it pours, though,
when the heavens open, the clouds burst
and the deluge descends.
Then the dabbing, dotting, damping
turns to streaming and teaming,
torrenting and henting, pouring and
squalling, flurrying and fissing.

It comes down in so many ways;
in sheets or by chucking and luttering,
siling or tipping or plothering.

Or perhaps, it may simply piss it down.

Still, nice weather for ducks.

Without You

without you
my life in darkness passes
i fall down deep crevasses

oh i miss you masses

how i hate it
when i lose my glasses

Poundland Economics

If I had a pound
for every Poundland
I have seen,
I would have enough money
to buy one item
in every Poundland
I have seen.

Two Paths Diverged

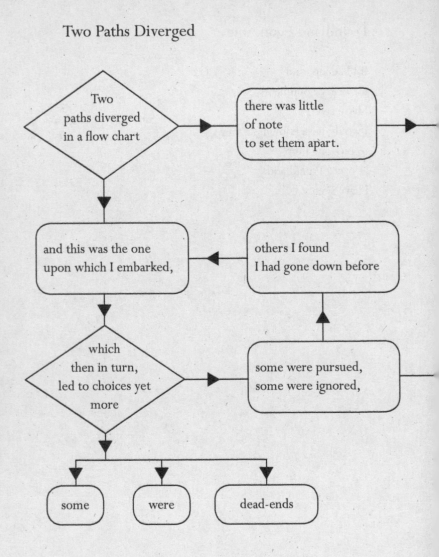

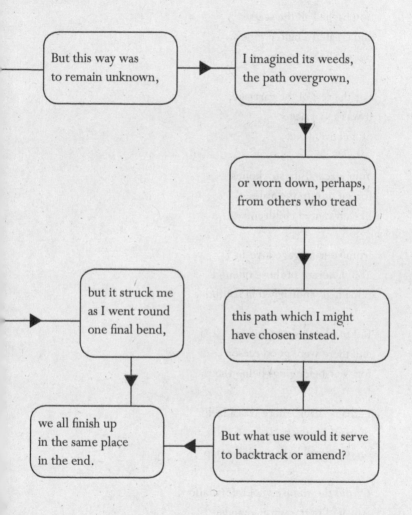

But this way was
to remain unknown,

I imagined its weeds,
the path overgrown,

or worn down, perhaps,
from others who tread

this path which I might
have chosen instead.

but it struck me
as I went round
one final bend,

But what use would it serve
to backtrack or amend?

we all finish up
in the same place
in the end.

You Bagged All the Seats

You bagged all the seats
and created a buffer zone
out of all that you own.

For the rest of the carriage,
it was a marriage
of inconvenience.

Your stacked-up stockpiles
forced us into the aisles,
like unwanted children

from your luggage love-in.
You, ignorant of those queued,
remained sandbagged in solitude.

But maybe this was unfair
and there were good reasons
for your belongings being there.

Perhaps, alack, there was a lack
of space on the rack
or your tired bags needed a nap.

Or did they house vital information,
which, if in the wrong hands,
might bring down This Great Nation?

Or are you a tropical disease carrier
so you built this big bag barrier,
to prevent further cases?

Or maybe you're a crusader
for luggage equality?
BAGS HAVE RIGHTS LIKE YOU AND ME!

Or perhaps it is that
you are simply
a twat.

Over My Dead Body

I cut off my nose
to spite my face.

In revenge,
my face
took up arms
against my legs

and yet,
all the while,
my feet were killing me.

4×4

your	four	by	four
parked	outside	my	door
means	i	cannot	see
the	sky	no	more

please	don't	ask	me
to	show	some	pity
you	block	my	view
and	pollute	the	city

i	don't	know	what
you	need	one	for
unless	it's	tank	practice
in	case	of	war

it's	six	feet	high
and	ten	feet	wide
please	go	and	live
in	the	country	side

Why I Have Never Read *War and Peace*: Ten Excuses

   I I've always meant to read it;
      I really like the sound of it.
      I had set aside the nineties
      but never quite got round to it.

  II I won't read the first half.
      It's because I'm a pacifist.
      I hope one day it gets abridged
      but without all the nasty bits.

 III The print's too small to read;
      it makes my interest dwindle.
      I tried to read the ebook
      but it was too big for my Kindle.

 IV I'm afraid it's not for me.
      I loved Tolstoy 1, 2 and 3,
      but I won't read this because
      there is no Woody or Buzz.

   V I think I left it on the bus.
      Or perhaps my dog ate it –
      although it may have been the cat
      (she thinks Tolstoy's overrated).

 VI I've been stuck
      on the first line
      since nineteen ninety-nine.

VII One day I'm sure I'll read it.
That has always been the plan.
But my concentration wavers
and I have a short attention Spanish omelette? Fabulous.

VIII I find it too weighty.
I feel like I'm eighty.
It's not so much the length,
I just don't have the strength
to read more than a page in a sitting.
Some say it's unputdownable,
but unpickupable is more fitting.

IX I would like to read it;
I really have the itch.
But the characters' names
all sound the same
and I won't know vich is vich.

X I fully intend to start it soon;
it is just a matter of when.
For the last ten years
I've been reading around it:
the jacket, the blurb, the ISBN.

Pretty Things

They spent the day swapping
stardust-sprinkled stories

of classroom rebel rebels
and rescued car journeys,

eye-shadowed evenings
of first gigs and girlfriends,

best gigs and boyfriends,
fan letters insanely penned,

awkward teenage oddities,
faces and phases and changes,

moon landings, all-time lows,
serendipity in far-off places,

the loneliness of Lazarus,
and the golden years of families,

fame, fashion, fancies, dances,
all the fanatically-vinyled panoplies,

tall, true tales of we-can-be-heroes,
for Planet Earth was blue

and there was nothing else
they could do.

The Love Song of Brian H. Bilston

La belle Una Stubbio, flicki-kicki subbuteo,
Lei è molto bella, charade di muteo.

Let us go then, you and I,
when I have finished this mushroom pie
and cleared away the table.
Let us go, through sterile shopping malls,
consumer cathedrals
of bargain baskets in Poundshop aisles
and cut-price calendars of Harry Styles,
to lead you to an underwhelming question ...
Oh, do not ask, 'What are you on about?'
Let us go and work it out.

In the room the women come and go
talking of Barry Manilow.

And indeed there will be time
for selfies in fast-food restaurant toilets,
or dirtied department store changing rooms;
there will be time, there will be time
to prepare your face for Instagram;
there will be time for Facebook and for Twitter,
and time for all your life's minutiae
to be spread like butter across the sky,
time for blackjack in the new casino
before the taking of a frappuccino.

In the room the women come and go
talking of Paolo di Canio.

And indeed there will be time
to wonder, 'Do I care?' and, 'Do I care?'
Time to turn back and listen to Cher,
with my newly grown facial hair—
(They will say: 'Throw his pipe into a bin!')
My frayed tank top, wearing thin,
the quadrupling of my double chin—
(They will see the fade of tattoos upon my skin.)

I should have been a piece of unsuspected lego
embedding myself into the soles of yellowed feet.

I grow old ... I grow old ...
I shall subscribe to UK Comedy Gold.
Shall I become thin and frail? Do I dare to eat some kale?
Regardless, I will always hate the *Daily Mail*.
I have heard the boy bands singing on the radio.
I do not think that they will sing to me.
I have seen them dancing on Saturday night talent shows
prowling the stage with their hair blown back
when the wind machine whirls and their jaws go slack.
We have suffered the agony of the buffering page,
lapsed into a sleeping silence, the uncomprehending frown,
till Katie Hopkins wakes us, and we drown.

Ceci N'est Pas un Poème

I wrote
some words

and made them look
like a poem

put line breaks

in
thought-provoking
places

but it was still

    just some words

and not
a poem

Acknowledgements

Thank you to the team at Unbound who have helped to put this book in your hands – it has been such a delightful experience – and especially to Scott Pack who somehow saw something in my poems to consider them worth publishing.

I have tested the forbearance of many around me over the last few years and, in particular, I would like to thank Kate Jaeger and Jake, George and Evie Millicheap for containing their anger (or boredom) with me during the writing of these poems.

I am indebted to Laura Montgomery and Louise Morgan for their consistently sound advice and encouragement. They should consider a career in publishing themselves.

And, of course, I owe a huge thank you to everyone who has helped to support this project: the fine people of Twitter and Facebook who took the time to read these poems in the first place, and the kind and generous souls whose names decorate the back of this book. This book simply could not have happened without you.

Brian Bilston

Supporters

Joe Abley
Carole Adams
Mark Adams
Matt Adams
Jon Adamson
Rusty Ahearne
Leah Alaani
Fiona Alderman
Charlie Alexander
Moose Allain
Margaret Allen
Paul Allen
Simon Allen
Angie Anderson
Colin Anderson
angelreader
Rich Ard
Meg Armstrong
Trevor Armstrong
Miffy Arnold
Jemma Arrowsmith
John Arthur
Liam Ashby
Ian Ashman
Kathryn Atkinson
Alister Babb
Liz Babb
Claire Bailey
Emma Balfe
Rob, Amy, James,
    & Ellie Bambridge
Adam Banks
Eleanor Banks

Amanda Banner
David Barfoot
Tracy Barlow
Ian Barnes
Gareth Barton
Matthew Bate
Rachel Beagley
Adele Beeken
George B. Bell
Emma Bennett
Anna Benson
Steven Benson
Lorna Berrett
Tim Beuzeval
Sarah Bird
Chloe Birr-Pixton
Rod Bissett
Carolyn Black
Alastair Block
Val Blunden
David Bolton
Iain Bonehill
Arie-Willem Bons
Cath Booth
Tim Boswell
Rachel Bowden
Jackie Bowles-Kay
Mike Boxall
Chris Boyd
Nicky Bramley
Carys Bray
Richard W H Bray
Jamie Breeze

Will Breitholtz
Andrew Brighton
David Brooks
Neil Broomfield
James Lupton Brown
Kate Quartano Brown
Vicki Brown
Matthew Brown
    (mattonethree)
Tiger and Dooster Bryce
Bingo Bumfudge
BunnyBrunnhilde
Jonny Bunt
Amanda Burley
Kenneth Burnett
Luke Burstow
Tom Burton
Jennifer Bush
Matt Buxton
Judy Buzzell
Martina BWC
Sue Byrne
T C
Chris Cafferty
Zoe Calvert
Ben Cameron
Ben Camm-Jones
Phillipa Candy
Marisa Cardoni
Mary Ann Carman
Philip Carpenter
Vivienne Carter
Beck Cartoons

G Carvajal
Brendan Casey
Michael Casey
Sally Cawdery
Heather Cawte
Gautam Chadda
Lynn Cherny
Paul Child
Sam Chodary
ChrisP
Jo Christie
Andrew Churchill
Claire Civil
Steve Clarricoats
Vivienne Clore
Rachel Clutterbuck
Julia Coffey
Angela Cohen
Jeremy Collins-White
Mick Conmy
Sarah Cook
Peter Coombe
Guy Cooper
Jason, Sophie, Santi and
     Eva-May Cooper
Piers Cooper
Caroline Corfield
Melanie Cotter
Andrew Cotterill
Deny Coughlan
Julia Cox
Leon Cox
Mrs Cox
Dave Craig
Iain Craig
Steven Craig

Simon Craven
Kim Crawford
Beth and Chris
     Cresswell
Alan Crossan
Donald Crowther
WInterfruit Crumblepie
Robert Cubitt
Shannon Cullen
Stan Cullimore
Michael Cunningham
Tom Curtis
J-F Cuvillier
Anne da Costa
Charlotte Dale
Tabitha Dale
Paul Davies
Paul Bassett Davies
James Davis
Tom Dawkins
Dan Dawson
Penny de la Plain
Martin Deas
Tim Deegan
Harry Deerin
Hugh Denholm
Patrick Denny
Ravindra Deo
Anthony Dhanendran
Dr Alison Diaper
Matthew Dickson
Toby Dignum
Gill Dinning
Andy Dolphin
Caroline Donfield
Patrick Donovan

@drmikefraser
Katie Drysdale
Jackie Duckworth
Sidia Dunmow
Christine Dunn
Alison Dunnett
Mark Durbin
Valerie Duskin
Alan Dutch
Ali Eastwood
Simon Eckley
Hilary Edgcombe
Matthew Egglestone
Håvar Ellingsen
Edric Ellis
David Elphick
Steve English
Soulla Tantouri Eriksen
Adam Errington
Dor Evans
PJ Evans
Thomas Everest-Dine
Simon Everett
Roya Ewing
Lydia Fairman
Ian Falconer
Peter Falconer
Stuart Farquhar
Jennifer Faulconbridge
James Faux
Margaret Fay
Mike Fenton
Liz Ferguson
Margaret Ferguson
Rachel Ferriman
Jane Fielding

Rosie Fiore
David Fisher
Martin Fitzgerald
Annemarie Flanagan
Alison Fogg
Lesley Foote
Emil Fortune
Graeme Forward
Anna Foster
Ed Fox
Isobel Frankish
Rupert Franklin
Sarah Franklin
Ben Franklyn
Ben Freeman
Chris Fry
Max Fulham
Jon Fuller
Louise Fullwood
Lesley Furneaux
Louise Gall
Natalie Galustian
Mark Gamble
Janet Gan
Ian Garrard
Justin Gau
Matt Gaventa
Nicholas Getaz
Bilal Ghafoor
Adrian Gibbs
Julie Gibson
Lizzie Gilbert
Mark Gilbert
Mark Gillies
Nina Gilman-Hawkes
Matthew Gilmartin

Bruce Gilmour
Giulia Giordano
Julian Girdham
Dominic Gittins
Richard Glibbery
Travis Glover
Maria Godebska
Eleanor Goldsmith
Chris Goodhead
HT Goody
Ola Gotkowska
Keith Grady
Ginny Graham
Patrick Graham
Ian Grainger
Shane Grant
Ian Gregg
John Greig
Brian Grierson
Jo Grieve
Simon Griew
Shaun Griffin
Michael Guilfoyle
Andria H
Joe H
Johanna Haban
Colin Hagreen
June Hall
Kate Hall
Chris Hallam
Gretel Hallett
Steven Hallmark
Beth Hammond
Michelle Hampson
Siobhan Hanna
Tim Hardy

Ian Harris
Dave & Sarah Harrison
Richard Harrison
Ruby Harrison
Nick Harvey
Terry Harvey
Wendy Harvey
Aline Hayes
Mel Haynes
Rob Haynes
Abbie Headon
Fran Healey
Alexandra Jean Hedge
Hedgehog Bookshop,
   Penrith
Sean Hegarty
John Henderson
Samantha Henney
Alan Hepburn
Paul Herring
Tim Hewett
Gwyneth Hibbett
Charlotte Hillier
David Hindmarsh
David Hinks
Jon Hird
Norma Ho
Scott Hoad
Bing Hobson
Matt Hodges
Justin Holland
Tim Hollingsworth
Gina Holloway
Shirley Honey
Amy Hopkinson
Nick Horn

Gill Hornby
Lisa Hallett Howard
Ann Howarth
Nicola Howell
Chris Howland-Harris
Kathy Hoyle
Lesley Hoyles
Donna Hughes
Ian Paul Hughes
Jonathan Hughes
Stephanie Hughes
Andy Humphries
Mark Hunt
Claire Hyde
G. P. Hyde
I'm Nick I am
Robert Insall
Alan Jackson
Becky Jaeger
Kate Jaeger
Michael Jaeger
Smita Jamdar
Andy James
Daniel James
Sarah James
Steve James
Alan Jarvis
Michael Jelley
JemLovesTea
Dave Jessup
Phil Jimmieson
Tristan John
Derek Johnson
Chris Jones
Helen Jones
Owen and Cerys Jones

Sian Jones
Alice Jorgensen
Gillian Kane
Karin
Andy Karran
Sara Kathleen
Oonagh Keating
Joe Kellard
David Kelly
Marian Keyes
Dan Kieran
Joachim Kindler
Rich King
Martin Kinoulty
Richard Kirby
Candide Kirk
Abbie Kirkwood
Philip Kisray
Michaela Knowles
Jonny Knoxville
Tessa Kok
Edward Komocki
Simon Koppel
Steve Krikler
Pierre L'Allier
Heidi LaBudde
Kevin Lack
David Laine
Glen Laker
Mary-Ellen Lane
Mark Lanigan
Neil Larsen
Shelley Lawson
Sean Leahy
Richard Lee
Adam Leedham

Grace Leete
Chloe Leila
Louise Leonard
Naomi Lepora
Sophie Lewis
Merc Locke
Julie Lodge
John & Christine Lomax
Cliff Lonsdale
Cherise Lopes-Baker
Charlie Louth
Mark Lowe
Rachel Lucey
Robert Lukaszewicz
Paul Luke
Lul Lulham
DeAndra Lupu
Anna Lyaruu
Mike Lynd
Barry Lyons
Mike Lythgoe
CK & CL Ma
David Macdonald
Grace MacFarlane
John Machin
Rebecca Mackay
Stuart Mackay-Thomas
Colin MacKenzie
Rory Mackenzie
Ally 'H' Macleod
Ruth MacMullen
Alasdair MacPherson
David Maddocks
Rachel Major
Nik Makepeace
Christopher Malvern

Star Man
@Funk_Pump
James Mansfield
Judy Mansfield
James Marley
Stephen Marsden
Chris Marsh
Dawn Marsh
Jane Marshall
Alistair Martin
David Martin
Ian Martin
Paul Martin
Stuart Marven
Alexander Mason
Miriam Maus
Simon Mawdsley
Una McClean
Jane McClements
Rachel McComish
Alan McCrorie
Chris McCrudden
Karen McDonnell
Michelle McFadden
Pete McFarlane
Shane McGill
John McHale
Conor McKeown
Palma McKeown
Stuart McLachlan
Mark McLauchlan
Angus McLellan
Hilary McMahon
Amy McNece
Ela McSorley
Alec Meadows

Pip Meadway
Laura Meecham
Paul Meldrum
Joanne Mercer
Luke Merlini
Gail Miflin
The Milkchops of Kings Heath
Andy Millicheap
David Millicheap
Marlene Millicheap
Paul Millicheap
Jonathan Mills
Karen Mitchell
John Mitchinson
Gordon Moar
Edwin Moore
Kevin A. Moore
Trevor Moore
Stephen Morey
Mark Morfett
Dale Morgan
Louise Morgan
Vivienne Morgan
Kirsty Morris
Marie Morris
Oliver Morris
Tim Morris
Graham Moss
Ian Moules
Sue Moyce
Luke Murphy
Jenny Murray
Maggie Murray
Nick Murza
Caroline Myers

Lisa Nachtigall
Tom Nash
Carlo Navato
Geoff Naylor
Clare Newton
Alfred Ng
Hannah Nicholls
Julius Nicholson
Sarah Nicholson
Matthew Nobbs
Madeleine Norman
Dan North
Eleanor Nowill
David Nygren
Clodagh O Connor
Mike O'Brien
Rebecca O'Shea
Brett Oaten
Georgia Odd
Andrew Ormerod
Richard Osman
Harry Oulton
Susan Owens
Scott Pack
Ben Palentine
Siobhan Palmer
Susan Palmer
Lev Parikian
Jeff Parker
Tim Parkin
Janet Passmore
Graham Patrick
Cath Payne
Vicky Peakman
Bianca Pellet
Katie Penfold

Naomi Perilli
Adam Perry
Kate Pert
Dan Peters
Robert Phillips
Sean Pidgeon
Benedict Pinches
Jane Pink
Jonathan Pinnock
Hannah Platts
Louis Plowden-Wardlaw
Justin Pollard
Dan Pope
Libby Potter
Ann Poulsen
Martin Poulsen
The Poulsen Webbs
Tracy Powell
Chris Preece
Alex Preusser
Lee Price
Gareth Prior
Sarah Prior
Sam Proctor
PtheP PtheP
Zoe Pymer
Mr Roger Quimbly
Neil Quinn
Tom Quinn
David Ramsay
Nik Rawlinson
Steve Raywood
Jeannette Redmond
Malcolm Reed
Nick Reeve
Stewart Reid

Bernard Reilly
Terry Reynolds
Chris Richards
Ed Richards
Julia Richards
Andrew Richardson
Lucy Richardson
Rachel Richardson
Caroline Richmond
Wendy Richmond
Brenda Rigby
Susan Robertd
Ralph Roberts
Tony Roberts
Alan Robertshaw
Miss Susan Robin :)
Andrew Robins
Ruth Robinson
Andy Roden
Steve and Gill Roffey
Helen Rogers
Matthew Rooney
Katharine Roseveare
Martin
   & Lucas Raymond
Nicholas Ross
Gavin Rosser-Davies
Rebecca Rouillard
Brian Routledge
John Rowe
Maggie Rowe
Charlie Rowlands
David Rowlands
Papiya Russell
Stephen Sadler
Adam Sales

Barney Sampson
Gina Sanford
Catherine Santamaria
Kaye Savage
Alan Sawdon
Güntzel Schmidt
David Schneider
Rodney Schreiner
Colin Scott
Koen Sebregts
Katy Seel
Adrian Seeley
Zoe Seenan
Richard Seldon
Antonia Seymour
Wendy Shakespeare
Rebecca Sharp
Kathryn Sharples
Anna Shelton
Simon Shields
Sarah Sholl
Barry Short
Jonathan Shulman
Bartosz Siepracki
Claire Simmonds
Daniel Simon
Maggie Simpson
Joe Skade
@skillsmcgill
Andy Slusarczuk
Dr Steven D Smith
Emma Smith
Ian Smith
Jess Smith
Kate Smith
Rachel Smith

Richard Smith
Wendy Marie Smith
Mike Snare
Andrew Soar
Rachel Sommerville
Iain Spardagus
Barbara Spence
Laura Spira
Neil Starr
Rick Steele
Nick Stephens
Sarah Stevens
David Stokes
John Stokoe
Bill Stone
Rachael Stos-Gale
Douglas Streatfield
Rod Street
Matthew Strickland
Laura Stringer
Brendan Strong
Lynne Strutt
John Styles
Peter Su
Mary Sweeting
Rebecca T
Heather Tailby
Renée Takken
Penny Tattersall
Frances Taylor
Helen Taylor
James Taylor
Martin Taylor
Shereen Taylor
Chocolate Teapot
John Tebbutt

Dan Tedds
Dave Telford
Jez Templeton
Anna Tharia
Julian Thomas
Stewart Thomas
Mike Scott Thomson
Seth Thomson
Greg Tinker
Jonathan Tisdall
Gail Tomlin
Agnes Tomorrow
Richard Toner
Holly Tonks
Ben Townsend
Rob Townsend
Heather Trickey
Matthew Trigg
Katherine Trill
Toby Tripp
Martin Trotter
Stephen Trudgian
Andrew Tuft
Heather Tulip
Karen Turnbull
Neillsen Turner
Sherri Turner
Owen Tuz
Lisa Urquhart
Justin Vaughan
Helen Verity
Linda Verstraten &
    Pyter Wagenaar
Valentijn Veurtjes
Katrina Vines
Alice Violett

Ian Wacogne
Michael Wadding
Pete Waldron & Hilary
O'Donnell
Paul Walker
Susan Wall
Chris Wallbank
Ellen Wallenstein
Jayne Wallington
June Walmsley
Edward Walsh
Mick Walsh
Verity Warne
Jon Washbrook
Edward Wates
Harry Watson
James Watson
Richard Webber
Scott Weddell
Jess Weeks
Doreen Wells
Colin West
Dominic Weston
Marcy Wheeler
Sacha Wheeler
Hannah Whelan
Nicholas White
Andrew Whitehouse
Andrew Whitehurst
Alison Whitfield
Miranda Whiting
Becca Whittaker
Vicki Whittaker and
    Graeme Hayes
Will Wilcox
Amanda Wilkie

Simon Wilks
Benjamin Willard
David Williams
Elric Williams
Gary Williams
Jeremy Williams
Keith Williams
Roger Williams
Edward Williamson
Zoë-Elise Williamson
Claire Willis
Wendy Wilshaw
Amanda Wilson
Dora Wilson
Kirsten Wilson
Malcolm Wilson
Paul Wilson
Kate Winger ATH
Mark Winspear
Darren M Winter
Judith Edge Woodland
Susan Woodward
Laura Woolfson
Karen Wootton
Ann Worrall
Tamsin Wragg
Nick Wray
Andrew Wren
Chris Wright
Julia Wright
Stuart Wright
Gerald Wyatt
Steph Wyatt
Jonathan Wynne
Rebecca Yates

Avril York
Cromerty York
Martin Young
Ysanne Ysanne
Angela Zemp
Stephanie Zia

A Note About the Typefaces

This book is set in Perpetua, designed by Eric Gill
(1882–1940), an eccentric sculptor, printmaker, and
designer whose roots lay in the Arts and Craft move-
ment. It bears the designer's distinctive hand with its
chiselled, neo-classical quality that derives from Gill's
fondness for stone engraving.

In 1925 Stanley Morison commissioned Gill to design
a book face patterned after epigraphic, rather than
calligraphic, letters. Gill took some persuading to
take the work, in part due to his disdain for all things
mechanical, but given his increasing involvement with
the making of books at the Golden Cockerel Press, he
eventually agreed to the commission. And so began a
long, drawn-out design process – largely due to the
obstinate management of the Monotype hierarchy and
poor-quality work by UK punch-cutters.

Perpetua made its debut appearance, albeit without its
italic companion, in the first printing of Gill's collection
of essays, *Art-Nonsense*, printed and published by Hague
& Gill in 1929. The release of the typeface was finally
announced the following year, but Perpetua didn't
become generally available to the printing trade until
1932, several years after the original commission.

The title page is set in P22 Underground, based on
the original 1916 drawings by Edward Johnston for
London Underground, for which Gill, then an appren-
tice, executed some significant work. It remains the
primary type on signage across the whole of the
London transport network, including many bus stops.